Mental Reset

15-Day Devotional
Reset. Renew. Restore

D'Andrea Bolden

Bolden Publishing

Unless otherwise indicated, all scriptural quotations are from the *King James Version* of the Bible.

MENTAL RESET: 15-DAY DEVOTIONAL + JOURNAL

Bolden Publishing
P.O. Box 2025
Kalamazoo, MI 49003
boldenenterprisesllc@gmail.com

Reproduction of text in whole or in part without the written consent by the author is not permitted and is unlawful according to the 1976 United States Copyright Act.

Copyright © 2020 by D'Andrea Bolden

All Rights Reserved

Library of Congress of Cataloging-in Publication Data:

An application to register this book for cataloging has been submitted to the Library of Congress

First Edition

Printed in the United States of America

VISIT THE AUTHOR'S WEBSITE

WWW.DANDREABOLDEN.COM

TABLE OF CONTENTS

Day 1
Time for a Refreshing -1

Day 2
Reset Your Thinking -7

Day 3
Renew Your Mind -14

Day 4
Think on These Things -20

Day 5
Set Your Mind -26

Day 6
Guard Your Mind -32

Day 7
Speak Life Not Death -38

Day 8
Your Words Reveal Your Heart -44

TABLE OF CONTENTS

Day 9
The Need for a Clean Heart -50

Day 10
Overcoming Anger -56

Day 11
Overcoming Fear -63

Day 12
Overcoming Rejection -70

Day 13
Stop Worrying -77

Day 14
Time to Forgive -84

Day 15
Moving Forward -92

INTRODUCTION

One of the biggest battles we all fight is in our mind. Our mind can be a place of bondage and non-stop negativity. It is important for us to get our mind to a place that allows us to have a peaceful and prosperous life.

This is a short devotional to help assist you as you endeavor to shift your mindset. Shifting your mindset is important so that your entire life can change for the better. Allow this 15-day devotional to be a catalyst to a mental transformation. It's time for a Mental Reset!!!

As you begin this 15-day journey be sure to use the lined pages each day to write down your thoughts, favorite scriptures or other special notes. Each day there is an activity that will help you on your path as you adjust, upgrade, and shift your thinking.

As a companion to this book there is also a webpage that shares all things related to this devotional. I hope you enjoy this.

https://www.dandreabolden.com/mental-reset

Day 1

"Time for a Refreshing"

Acts 3:19-20a *"Repent therefore, and turn again, that your sins may be blotted out, that times of refreshing may come from the presence of the Lord,"*

One of the greatest lessons I have learned is that many times we need a refreshing. Refreshing is synonymous with new and fresh. The prefix re- means again so refreshing can be defined as making fresh or like new again.

Oftentimes as we go through life's ups, downs and many challenges it can begin to wear on our soul. As time passes you can go from excited and ready to take the world by storm to sad, isolated and feeling "blue".

Looking at the scripture above, for refreshing to come we first need to repent. Repenting is not an apology but rather a change of heart and going in the correct direction. You might need to repent for giving up, being lazy, complaining, falling into sin, being angry with God, or even just speaking negatively. Take the time to pray and in doing so repent and wait in His presence because only the Spirit of the living God can refresh you.

1. Repent
2. Ask the Lord to refresh you
3. Wait in His presence

Moments of Reflection

Moments of Reflection

Moments of Reflection

Moments of Reflection

Refresh

Activity # 1

Refocus your mind on the positive things in your life. Many times our minds focus on everything negative. God is better to us than we allow ourselves to think. Write a list of 10 things that you are grateful to the Lord for and then read the list out loud.

10 things that I am grateful for:

1. _____
2. _____
3. _____
4. _____
5. _____
6. _____
7. _____
8. _____
9. _____
10. _____

Day 2

"Reset your Thinking"

Philippians 4:18-19 *"Finally, brethren, whatever things are true, whatever things are noble, whatever things are just, whatever things are pure, whatever things are lovely, whatever things are of good report, if there is any virtue and if there is anything praiseworthy—meditate on these things. The things which you learned and received and heard and saw in me, these do, and the God of peace will be with you."*

How often have you found yourself agitated with a malfunctioning electronic device? Typically, when this happens you will shut the device down and restart it and if this does not work you might eventually reset the device to its original state.

Doing this type of reset will get rid of everything you have on the device and take it back to the bare minimum so that it is working at its best. Doing a reset frees up space and clears up anything that could be causing the device to malfunction.

Take this concept and apply it to your mind. Sometimes we have a lot of negative thought patterns and our minds are polluted and quite toxic. When this happens, you need to reset your thinking.

In order to reset your thinking, the first thing that you need to do is recognize the need to change your thinking. Your thinking can be so negative and so toxic for so long that you are used to it and it becomes normal. It takes time and effort to reset your thinking when you are accustomed to the same negative thought patterns. One suggestion to adjust your thinking is taking the time meditate on scriptures and even reading and speaking God's word out loud.

Moments of Reflection

Moments of Reflection

Moments of Reflection

Moments of Reflection

_____
_____
_____
_____
_____
_____
_____
_____
_____
_____
_____
_____
_____
_____
_____
_____
_____
_____
_____
_____

Reset

Activity # 2

Find some scriptures that you can meditate on daily. I personally like to use scriptures out of the book of Psalms, or other verses that remind me of God's goodness, His love, praising God etc. But please take the time and simply find scriptures that work for you.

My 10 scriptures to meditate on are:

1. _____
2. _____
3. _____
4. _____
5. _____
6. _____
7. _____
8. _____
9. _____
10. _____

Day 3

"Renew Your Mind"

Romans 12:2 *"And be not conformed to this world: but be ye transformed by the renewing of your mind, that ye may prove what is that good, and acceptable, and perfect, will of God."*

When you reset your mind, you have to be both intentional and consistent. It takes time and effort to line your mind up so that your thoughts are righteous and in agreement with the written Word of God.

The bible tells us to renew our minds. Renewing of the mind is one of the most important yet overlooked responsibilities of a believer. Every believer has mindsets, strongholds, and ungodly thinking patterns that must be overcome through the power of the Word.

The Word of God is the key to renewing your mind. Renew means to make new again. So, through the power of God's Word your mind can become new as you begin to line your thinking up with God's word. When a person change's their mind they have changed as a person.

1. Challenge yourself to read the word daily.
2. Pray the word daily.
3. Declare scriptures over your life daily.

Moments of Reflection

Moments of Reflection

Moments of Reflection

Moments of Reflection

Renew

Activity # 3

When you begin to pay closer attention to your thinking and the things you dwell on in your mind you might uncover procrastination, making excuses, fear, worry, sadness, unforgiveness, lust or even anger. Out of everything mentioned making excuses is one that many people battle with. Some people make excuses to avoid certain situations while other people might make excuses when they do not want to do something.

Using the space below I want you to write down the top excuses that you are going to stop making going forward. Be sure to look back at this page to hold yourself accountable.

Excuses I will no longer make going forward

1. _____
2. _____
3. _____
4. _____
5. _____
6. _____
7. _____
8. _____
9. _____

Day 4

"Think on These Things"

Philippians 4:8 *"'Finally, brothers, whatever is true, whatever is honorable, whatever is just, whatever is pure, whatever is lovely, whatever is commendable, if there is any excellence, if there is anything worthy of praise, think about these things."*

Oftentimes, if we are honest we can admit to ourselves and others that our thinking can be rather negative. Our thinking affects our mood and even our behavior. So, if we want to change for the better it begins with our mind.

Every day you have to work on your thoughts becoming more and more like Philippians 4:8. I have found for myself that when I think about things that fit the scripture above I feel better. Many times when I felt down in the dumps my thoughts were right down there with me.

Changing your thinking is honestly one of the hardest things that you will have to do. It takes consistency and effort to fill your mind with the types of things the Lord wants us to think about on a regular basis.

1. Post scriptures in your house
2. Listen to Christian music and sermons throughout the week.
3. Find uplifting Christian podcasts and books.
4. Meditate on scriptures
5. Read scriptures out loud
6. Daily Biblical affirmations

Moments of Reflection

Moments of Reflection

Moments of Reflection

Moments of Reflection

Thoughts

Activity # 4

What are some things that you are currently praying about? (i.e. health, breakthrough, wisdom etc.).

Things that I am praying for:

1. _____
2. _____
3. _____
4. _____
5. _____
6. _____
7. _____
8. _____
9. _____
10. _____

Day 5

"Set Your Mind"

Romans 8:5-6 *"For those who live according to the flesh set their minds on the things of the flesh, but those who live according to the Spirit set their minds on the things of the Spirit. For to set the mind on the flesh is death, but to set the mind on the Spirit is life and peace."*

Did you know that what you set (focus) your mind on governs the way you live your life? Your mindset will either guide you to live according to your flesh or the Spirit. According to the scripture your mindset will lead to death, or life and peace.

When your mind is set on something you become mentally focused or even consumed by that very thing. As believers we need to focus and dedicate our mind on the things of the Spirit. This is what yields life and peace in our lives. If you find yourself lacking peace take a moment and consider what your mind has been set or dwelling on.

1. Pray and ask God to help you set your mind on the things of the Spirit.
2. Recognize when your mind is focused on the wrong things and shift your focus.
3. Combat negative thinking with gratefulness

Moments of Reflection

Moments of Reflection

Moments of Reflection

Moments of Reflection

My mind

Activity # 5

What are the scriptures that help keep you encouraged during difficult seasons of your life?

Scriptures that encourage me:

1. _____
2. _____
3. _____
4. _____
5. _____
6. _____
7. _____
8. _____
9. _____
10. _____

Day 6

"Guard Your Mind"

2 Corinthians 10:5 *"We destroy arguments and every lofty opinion raised against the knowledge of God, and take every thought captive to obey Christ,"*

Our thought life can be like a runaway train. If we are not careful we will entertain and dwell on every thought that comes to our mind. The thought life of many people is not only very negative but also very undisciplined.

In order to take every thought captive we have to begin to be conscious and attentive as it relates to our thought life. This means recognizing the source of our thoughts along with identifying toxic thought patterns.

Some of things that randomly "pop" in our mind are thoughts, ideas, and suggestions from the enemy. It is important to remember that our mind is the battlefield. If the enemy can get control of your mind he can get control of you. This is because your thoughts, emotions and behaviors work together.

One way we filter or guard our mind is by filtering our life. This includes conversations, things we watch on television, books that we read, and music that we listen to on a regular basis. We cannot fill our minds with things that are ungodly and wonder why our minds do not line up with the Word of God.

Moments of Reflection

Moments of Reflection

Moments of Reflection

Moments of Reflection

Thinking

Activity # 6

What are some prayer points that you currently have? Do not overthink this your prayer point can be as simple as praying to the Lord to give you peace in your mind.

Prayer Points

1. _____
2. _____
3. _____
4. _____
5. _____
6. _____
7. _____
8. _____
9. _____
10. _____

Day 7

"Speak Life not Death"

Proverbs 18:21 *"Death and life are in the power of the tongue: and they that love it shall eat the fruit thereof."*

Our Heavenly Father is the creator of the universe and all that is in it. He created everything by speaking it into existence. And because we are created in His image we have the ability to speak words that will yield a harvest.

Our words are like seeds and with any seed you will reap a harvest based on what was sown. We must be careful in knowing that words are powerful seeds that have meaning and when we speak those words, we will yield a harvest. If you use your mouth to speak and declare blessings, deliverance, breakthrough or even healing you should have faith that those things will happen. On the other hand if you constantly speak defeat, loss, or negativity you should expect to receive a harvest from those seeds as well.

You have the power to change your entire life based on what you speak!

1. Declare blessings, favor and breakthrough over your life.
2. Speak life every single day!
3. Do not allow discouragement or even anger to cause you to speak negative words over your life.
4. Use your mouth to speak blessings over others.

Moments of Reflection

Moments of Reflection

Moments of Reflection

Moments of Reflection

_____
_____
_____
_____
_____
_____
_____
_____
_____
_____
_____
_____
_____
_____
_____
_____
_____
_____
_____
_____

Speak Life

Activity # 7

Speak Life

Write down at least 10 biblical affirmations for your life.

1. _____
2. _____
3. _____
4. _____
5. _____
6. _____
7. _____
8. _____
9. _____
10. _____

Day 8

"Your Words Reveal Your Heart"

Matthew 15:10 *"What goes into someone's mouth does not defile them, but what comes out of their mouth, that is what defiles them."*

Did you know that your very words can defile you? When considering the scriptures above Jesus had to make it plain to the people that it is not food that will defile you but the very words that you speak.

When something is defiled it means that it has become violated, contaminated or even polluted. Our words have the ability to contaminate us. Speak God's Word and speak life.

Luke 6:45 *"A good man out of the good treasure of his heart bringeth forth that which is good; and an evil man out of the evil treasure of his heart bringeth forth that which is evil: for of the abundance of the heart his mouth speaketh."*

Ultimately what a person speaks is a clear reflection of their heart. I am pretty sure just about everyone has heard someone say, "I did not mean to say that". Although they might regret what they said or even the consequences that follow, those words still came from their heart. This is why a clean heart is so important because your words reveal your heart.

1. Think before you speak
2. Don't allow yourself to release words from a place of anger or bitterness.

Moments of Reflection

Moments of Reflection

Moments of Reflection

Moments of Reflection

Words

Activity # 8

Think of all the areas of your life that need improvement. (i.e. relationships, time management, financial discipline, exercise, temper etc.). Then consider what the word says and write biblical declarations.

Ex: According to Deut 8:18 God I thank you for giving me the power to create [establish] wealth.

Write biblical declarations over those areas.

1. _____
   _____

2. _____
   _____

3. _____
   _____

4. _____
   _____

5. _____
   _____

Day 9

"The Need for a Clean Heart"

Psalm 51:10 *"Create in me a clean heart, O God; and renew a right spirit within me."*

As believers it is important that we ask the Lord to cleanse our heart. Our motives, desires, and even our attitudes stem from our heart.

Everything that we say from our lips comes from our heart. The heart is also where sin is conceived. This is why Jesus explained how one can commit adultery in their heart. Because what is in your heart will eventually manifest.

Proverbs 4:23 *"Above all else, guard your heart, for everything you do flows from it."*

Psalm 24:3-4 *"Who may ascend the mountain of the LORD? Who may stand in his holy place? The one who has clean hands and a pure heart, who does not trust in an idol or swear by a false god."*

We have to be honest in realizing that no one truly knows our heart but God. We can even believe that our heart is right and be blinded to our own heart. This is why it is important to ask God to reveal and cleanse our heart.

1. Ask the Lord to show you your own heart.
2. Ask the Lord to give you a clean and pure heart.

Jeremiah 17:9 *" The heart is deceitful above all things, and desperately wicked: who can know it?"*

Moments of Reflection

Moments of Reflection

Moments of Reflection

Moments of Reflection

Clean Heart

Activity # 9

Find scriptures that reference the state of one's heart: (ex. Matthew 6:21)

List your scriptures below.

1. _____
2. _____
3. _____
4. _____
5. _____
6. _____
7. _____
8. _____
9. _____
10. _____

Day 10

"Overcoming Anger"

Ephesians 4:26: *Be ye angry, and sin not: let not the sun go down upon your wrath:*

Anger: a strong feeling of annoyance, displeasure, or hostility. {ref: oxford dictionary online}

The Lord designed for us to have emotions. So, the concept of anger itself is not the issue but rather how we respond when we are angry. Do you get angry and begin to cuss, fight, or even destroy and vandalize things?

Anger is typically the result of something that has happened. But it becomes problematic based on our behavior and if we stay angry for long periods of time. It would be normal to get angry if you were slapped in the face by a stranger. But to remain angry for a very long period of time is a problem. We are not created to stay angry for long periods of time. In fact, there are studies that have proven how anger over time can negatively affect your health.

The inability to properly process anger can result in a lot of issues that will spill over into relationships, employment, parenting, ministry, physical and even mental health. The ability to get angry but not sin or stay angry is a must for believers.

1. Meditate on scriptures related to joy, love and peace
2. Spend time listening to soaking music and worship music.

3. Pray and ask God to deliver you from the spirit of anger and to help you.
4. Begin to recognize when you feel yourself getting angry in order to change the way you would normally respond.
5. Consider professional Christian counseling to help you get to the root and heal.

Moments of Reflection

Moments of Reflection

Moments of Reflection

Moments of Reflection

I am Happy

Activity # 10

Think of the happiest memories in your life and write them down. This doesn't have to be anything big it can be simple things such as your first job, your first car, graduating high school etc.

1. _____
2. _____
3. _____
4. _____
5. _____
6. _____
7. _____
8. _____
9. _____
10. _____

Day 11

"Overcoming Fear"

2 Timothy 1:7 *"For God hath not given us the spirit of fear; but of power, and of love, and of a sound mind."*

1 John 4:18 *"There is no fear in love; but perfect love casteth out fear: because fear hath torment. He that feareth is not made perfect in love."*

Fear: an unpleasant emotion caused by the belief that someone or something is dangerous, likely to cause pain, or a threat. {ref: oxford dictionary online}

Fear can take many forms such as; fear of the dark, fear of failure, fear of rejection or even fear of demons. Contrary to the definition listed above a person can be fearful of something that is in no way a possible physical danger (dolls, aluminum foil, clocks etc).

Fear is crippling, the anticipation of that which is feared can completely paralyze a person. People have the tendency to behave in way that allows them to avoid the source of their fear even if it is very unlikely to occur or ever cause them harm (i.e. fear of being eaten by a clown, fear of aluminum foil)

The root of control and much anxiety in the lives of some people is simply fear. God does not want the spirit of fear to cripple and plague the lives of His people. The spirit of fear wants people to feel powerless, to feel a lack of love and not have a sound mind. According to the scripture above the remedy for fear is not courage but love (ref: 1 John 4:18). God's love will break the power of fear.

1. Pray for the Lord to perfect you in love.
2. Take your anxiety and fear and give it to the Lord.
3. Pray for God's peace to fill your heart.
4. Fast and pray for the spirit of fear to be broken off your life.
5. Consider professional Christian counseling to help you get to the root and heal.

Moments of Reflection

Moments of Reflection

Moments of Reflection

Moments of Reflection

Fearless

Activity # 11

Dump the junk!

What are somethings that you need to let go of? Sometimes we need to evaluate our lives and realize we have too many unnecessary things that are not helping us.

Do not overthink this it can be as simple as watching less TV or deciding to forgive an offense. You might need to break bad habits or be on social media less. Take a moment and think of things that you can get rid of in your life.

1.
2.
3.
4.
5.
6.
7.
8.
9.
10.

Day 12

"Overcoming Rejection"

Isaiah 53:3 *"He is despised and rejected of men; a man of sorrows, and acquainted with grief: and we hid as it were our faces from him; he was despised, and we esteemed him not."*

No one knows rejection like our Lord and Savior, Jesus Christ. A lot of people can relate feeling rejected over everyday occurrences but can you imagine sacrificing your very life for people that reject you?

Rejection will happen in life but you do not have to be bound by the spirit of rejection. The power of rejection can begin to break when you realize that your worth is not tied to rejection or acceptance by man. When I look at the rejection Christ experienced and overcame it makes the rejection I have experienced seem rather trivial.

Rejection is never a good feeling in fact rejection if not handled properly can cause us to reject ourselves and even others. Unresolved issues related to rejection can be at the root of low self-esteem and even the inability to properly give and receive love. Rejection can make it hard for you to build and maintain healthy relationships.

There are some things you can do to help you begin to overcome rejection.

1. Read scriptures that speak of God's love for you
2. Find scriptures that emphasize your divine makeup

3. Find scriptures that reaffirm your unique God given purpose.
4. Find scriptures that deepen your understanding of God's love.
5. Learn to love and value yourself.
6. Consider professional Christian counseling to help you get to the root and heal.

Moments of Reflection

Moments of Reflection

Moments of Reflection

Moments of Reflection

Loved by God

Activity # 12

Look beyond yourself

It is always a rewarding feeling when you take the focus off of yourself and consider others. I don't mean this in an unhealthy way. But sometimes we can be so self-centered we do not consider others.

Take the time to think of other people that you can pray for. It can be people you know, people in governmental positions, you can pray for other nations and so forth.

1.
2.
3.
4.
5.
6.
7.
8.
9.
10.

Day 13
"Stop Worrying"

Although it is easier said than done it is imperative that as believers we are not plagued by constant worrying. Constant worry causes a lack of peace in our lives. Honestly, can we say we truly trust God if we are worried about every small detail of our lives? Do we really believe His Word if thoughts of worry are in our minds constantly?

Fear and the inability to control every aspect of our lives 24/7 can perpetuate worry in our lives. In other words we can find ourselves worried about things that "could" go wrong or worried about things that are beyond our control.

Worry is not of God. Our Heavenly Father wants us to have the same peace that is mentioned in His Word. He does not want His children in a constant state of panic and worry. Let's look at what the Bible says about God's peace. Because peace and real trust in God is what the constant worrier needs in his or her life.

Colossians 3:15- Let the peace of Christ rule in your hearts, since as members of one body you were called to peace. And be thankful.

Galatians 5:22 - But the fruit of the Spirit is love, joy, peace, forbearance, kindness, goodness, faithfulness,

Philippians 4:6-7 - Do not be anxious about anything, but in every situation, by prayer and petition, with thanksgiving, present your requests to God. ⁷ And the peace of God, which transcends all understanding, will guard your hearts and your minds in Christ Jesus.

Moments of Reflection

Moments of Reflection

Moments of Reflection

Moments of Reflection

God's Peace

Activity # 13

Prayer + Scripture Challenge

Challenge yourself to shift your mind towards the Lord in prayer and in His Word. Every time you have down time that you would normally spend scrolling on social media or watching TV take a few minutes and read a scripture and pray the Word back to the Father.

Try to keep track of how many times you pray and read scripture by writing down the times you do this throughout the day.

____ : _____ am or pm

____ : _____ am or pm

____ : _____ am or pm

____ : _____ am or pm

____ : _____ am or pm

____ : _____ am or pm

____ : _____ am or pm

____ : _____ am or pm

____ : _____ am or pm

____ : _____ am or pm

Day 14

"Time to Forgive"

One thing I have found to be common both in and out of the church is unforgiveness. A lot of people have experienced some very painful situations and refusing to forgive is the response of a lot people. When hurt and pain is not resolved a person can harbor anger and resentment while becoming very bitter in their heart.

Professionals have begun to recognize that unforgiveness can have a negative impact on your health. This is where therapy comes in to help people work through and resolve these issues so that they are able to forgive the offense and the offender.

The road to healing and forgiveness is not the same for everyone especially for individuals that deal with the aftermath of traumatic events. These people might deal with insomnia, nightmares related to the traumatic event, flash backs or other common symptoms related to trauma.

Although forgiving is not always easy it is necessary. The bible states emphatically that if we do not forgive others God will not forgive us. Unforgiveness can cause us to miss out on the blessings and favor of God. Don't miss your breakthrough and your destiny holding on to offense and unforgiveness.

Some of the reasons I find people do not want to forgive is because they feel that is letting the person off the hook and that is simply not true. Or they feel that forgiving means that everything goes back to normal.

Forgiveness does not mean a person is not guilty of wrong-doing. For instance, if someone stole your life savings would you want this person to hold your wallet and have a key to your house? You must forgive but you should not put yourself in a position to be hurt in the same manner again.

Forgiveness does not mean the person was not wrong or does not need to face consequences. Forgiveness does not mean you automatically trust a person again. Forgiveness does not mean you will have any type of relationship with the person.

Forgiveness means that you have released the offense and the offender from your heart. Forgiveness means that you are no longer harboring anger and resentment. Forgiveness means that you have obeyed scripture. Forgiveness means that you are FREE!!!

Ephesians 4:31-32 – *Get rid of all bitterness, rage and anger, brawling and slander, along with every form of malice. Be kind to one another, tenderhearted, forgiving one another, as God in Christ forgave you.*

Mark 11:25 – *And whenever you stand praying, forgive, if you have anything against anyone, so that your Father also who is in heaven may forgive you your trespasses."*

Colossians 3:13 – *Bearing with one another and, if one has a complaint against another, forgiving each other; as the Lord has forgiven you, so you also must forgive.*

John Hopkins Medicine: Forgiveness Your Health Depends On It
https://www.hopkinsmedicine.org/health/wellness-and-prevention/forgiveness-your-health-depends-on-it

1. Consider professional Christian counseling to help you get to the root and heal.

Moments of Reflection

Moments of Reflection

Moments of Reflection

Moments of Reflection

I Can Forgive

Activity # 14

What is important to you?

Have you ever thought about what is most important to you? What do you value the most in life? Today you will create a list that will show the things that are not only important to you but that are probably also a priority.

List the ten most important and valuable factors in your life. This can be people, places, and things.

1.
2.
3.
4.
5.
6.
7.
8.
9.
10.

Day 15

"Moving Forward"

Progress comes partially from discipline and consistency. It takes time to shift your mindset for the better. The goal is not just for you to go through this devotional but for you to apply the things that work well for you.

Life is a journey that requires effort and hard work. The inability to make wise decisions, live by biblical principles, and stay focused are what typically contribute to people not getting what they want out of life.

In the Word of God we see where wisdom, knowledge, and understanding are all mentioned. Knowledge is simply information. Understanding is comprehension of the information. Wisdom is the application of the information that you can comprehend. For many people wisdom or simply knowing what to do is what is lacking.

You can no longer afford to go to webinars, read books, attend conferences and still remain stagnant and fruitless in your life. The ability to move forward can require that you use wisdom and apply biblical principles to your life.

Moments of Reflection

Moments of Reflection

Moments of Reflection

Moments of Reflection

I Have Joy

Activity # 15

In order to have the life you want you will have to put hard work and effort in to make it happen. Discipline, time management, organization, well-defined goals, and consistent effort can and will yield results.

Once you take the time to clear you mind of the clutter and unplug yourself from life's unnecessary busyness. This activity has two parts; the first is time management and the second is goals.

#1 Time Management

Do you know where you time goes on a regular basis? People that don't manage their time will always say they don't have enough time. There are 7 days in a week and 24 hours in one day so every week you have 168 hours to manage. I want you to list everything you do in a week and how many hours you spend doing each activity. Try to account for as many hours as possible include things such as sleeping, working, cooking, cleaning but base the number of hours on one week.

Good time management will allow you to maximize your time and not waste it or make excuses. You will need good time management in order to achieve your goals and get your life to the next level.

Use the space below to write down how many hours you typically spend on various tasks every week. You will record the hours based on a week so 8 hours of sleep per day would be recorded as 56 hours/week. Also, you want to try and account for as much time as possible and get as close to 168 hours {there are 168 hours in a week)

i.e.   40 hours – work, 56 hours – sleep, 8 hours – TV

Hours/week	Activity

#2 Goals

Your goals should lead you in the direction you want your life to go. Some goals are short term and others are longer. Many times are short term goals are pre-cursors to our long term goals.

It is not enough to simply write our goals down on paper but you also need action steps. Action steps are the things you need to do to accomplish a specific goal. This ensures you are on track to achieve your goals and progress on a continuous basis. You can record you goals on the next page.

List 3 goals and the steps needed to accomplish each particular goal.

Goal # 1_____

    1.

    2.

    3.

    4.

    5.

Goal # 2_____

    1.

    2.

    3.

    4.

    5.

Goal # 3_____

    1.

    2.

    3.

    4.

    5.

Moments of Reflection

Moments of Reflection

Moments of Reflection

Moments of Reflection

I Am Blessed

www.ingramcontent.com/pod-product-compliance
Lightning Source LLC
Chambersburg PA
CBHW020428010526
44118CB00010B/471